THE LAST DAYS OF STEAM IN
DEVON

To St Budeaux Railway Circle, who, although now scattered around the country, have taken many of the photographs in this volume (Mike Daly, Terry Nicholls, Larry Crosier and Maurice Dart)

THE LAST DAYS OF STEAM IN
DEVON

– MAURICE DART –

ALAN SUTTON

First published in the United Kingdom in 1991 by
Alan Sutton Publishing Ltd · Phoenix Mill · Stroud · Gloucestershire

Copyright © Maurice Dart 1991

British Library Cataloguing in Publication Data

Dart, Maurice
The last days of steam in Devon.
I. Title
625.26109425

ISBN 0-86299-925-1

Endpapers: Front: A Penzance engine, 4500 class 2–6–2T 4566, leaves Torquay on 20.7.60 with the 8.10 p.m. Newton Abbot–Paignton. This was the last steam loco officially to be repaired at Newton Abbot factory, leaving there on 15.7.60.

Peter Gray

Back: Newton Abbot West signal-box is behind 2884 2–8–0 2887 of Severn Tunnel Junction shed which is heading an 'Up' freight past the station on 14.6.61.

Peter Gray

Typeset in Palatino 9/10
Typesetting and origination by
Alan Sutton Publishing Limited
Printed and bound in Great Britain by
Butler & Tanner Ltd, Frome and London

Introduction

Devon, the second largest county in England, was served by the Great Western and the Southern Railways, each following routes which differed greatly in character. For many years after nationalization there was still a definite 'company' atmosphere around most of the system with branch trains on the GWR known as 'auto-workings' and on the SR as 'motor-trains'.

Plymouth and Exeter were served by both lines. The GWR followed a southerly route around Dartmoor which entailed heavy engineering works, with viaducts crossing river valleys and tunnels at the top of the famous South Devon Banks at Dainton and Tigley/Rattery. These gradients together with Hemerdon near Plympton required all heavy trains between Plymouth and Newton Abbot to be 'double-headed' or in the case of freight trains, assisted in the rear by a 'banker'. Awe-inspiring spectacles and sounds to excite railway enthusiasts, but very hard sweat and graft for the firemen on the engines, and the driver, coaxing their charges, blasting up the banks and through the woods, which in the autumn delivered another hazard – falling leaves on rails already slippery with rain. The line from the Torbay area, which generated heavy holiday traffic, joined just before Newton Abbot, which used to be a mecca for railway lovers, then on to Exeter passing the scenic stretch through the 'Rock Tunnels' – superb in the summer, but notorious in winter storms at high tides, when the waves splash up over passing trains and at times break the sea wall near Parson's tunnel and at Dawlish. Branch lines full of character served inland towns, with others heading for the coast.

The SR followed the River Tamar and skirted the western and northern slopes of Dartmoor on easier gradients, with a summit at Sourton, a grim area in the depth of winter, to reach Okehampton, with its station perched high on the hillside above the town, rarely windless and often rainswept. This was the Junction station for the lines to North Cornwall via Halwill, where four lines met, the one to Torrington and Bideford being a railway enthusiasts delight but a financial disaster to the operating department, with passengers normally numbering six at the most. Then along the river to Barnstaple, the Junction for the hilly line to Ilfracombe, and the twin routes south, to Yeoford and Taunton through wooded river valleys. At Yeoford the two SR lines joined to curve gently alongside rivers to reach Exeter St David's, where the incline of 1 in 37 up to Exeter Central required assistance. To see and hear a heavy ballast train from Meldon Quarry, often with four or five engines, tackle this was an experience – two Ns with two E1/Rs and an M7 all working flat out.

Exeter always presented a problem to enthusiasts regarding which station to spend most time at: St David's with its 'Kings', 'Castles' and 'Halls', or Central with its

'Merchant Navys', 'West Countrys' and 'King Arthurs'. Beyond Exeter, with its large engine shed at Exmouth Junction, the SR threw off a succession of branch lines to the coast running through pastoral and wooded country.

Much of this is now history as both the GW and SR have been pruned. The GWR lost its branch lines apart from Paignton and intermediate stations between Plymouth and Totnes closed, with diesels gradually replacing steam traction from 1959. The SR was cut brutally with its main line being severed beyond Bere Alston with no passengers between Yeoford and Okehampton. The line to Barnstaple has survived but many branch lines were closed, leaving only that to Exmouth. Surprisingly main-line diesels appeared on the SR east of Exeter in the early 1950s for a few years, but steam returned only to be finally ousted from 1965 onwards, following transfer to the Western Region.

This book, it is hoped, will awaken memories of the activity at North Road, Newton Abbot, St David's and Central, the branch-line byways of both railways and the engine sheds at Laira, Newton, Exeter, Okehampton, Barnstaple Junction, Exmouth Junction and Friary. GWR 4–6–0s are depicted at work on the main line with pannier tanks, 'Prairies', and 0–4–2Ts on the branches.

SR 'Pacifics' are shown with a variety of tank locos on the branch lines, including BR types which replaced the ageing SR engines and SR and BR 4–6–0s and the faithful Ns and Us, which together with the T9s handled much of the SR traffic in Devon.

No longer does the Teign Valley echo to those sounds – specific to the GWR – of a tank loco free-wheeling, or stopped in a station and 'blowing a raspberry', nor can we hear the stirring shriek of a T9's whistle as it barked away from Bere Ferrers; long may these treasured memories remain with us.

Preservationists operate the Dart Valley and Torbay lines using GWR steam locos and there is talk of re-opening from Bere Alston to Tavistock and possibly from Yeoford to Okehampton. The Plym Valley line is an embryo preservation group on a short section of the GWR Tavistock branch at Marsh Mills, so through the county, a little of what was lost is being retrieved.

Maurice Dart

Acknowledgements

I would like to thank all those who have helped me with the preparation of this book and in particular Mike Daly for placing his negatives at my disposal for me to make a selection and later attempt to trace dates and details in diaries, still stowed away after several house moves; and Eric Youldon of Exeter for going through and extracting relevant photographs from the collection of his friend, the late Peter Tunks.

For supplying photographs and/or giving consent to use them I would like to thank Harry Cowan, Larry Crosier, John Gronwalt, Peter Gray, Alistair Jeffery, the late Arthur Luxton, Lens of Sutton, Michael Messenger, Richard Murrin, Terry Nicholls, the late Cedric Owen, Denis Richards, the late Roy Sambourne, John Scrace and Western Morning News Newspapers Ltd.

My thanks also go to: Larry Crosier and Edgar Whitear (both retired railwaymen) for information over the years; shedmasters and foremen at Laira, Newton Abbot, Exeter, Friary, Barnstaple Junction and Exmouth Junction; Richard Woodley for help in identifying some trains; Mike Blake for drawing the map; Walter Julian for proof reading with me; Tom Corin (Mid-Cornwall Photographic Services) for reprinting negatives and copying photographs; Emily Hancock for allowing me to turn her dining-room into a study while preparing this book; and Sarah Powell (Mayday Secretaries) for deciphering my writing, typing the manuscript and preparing the word-processing disc.

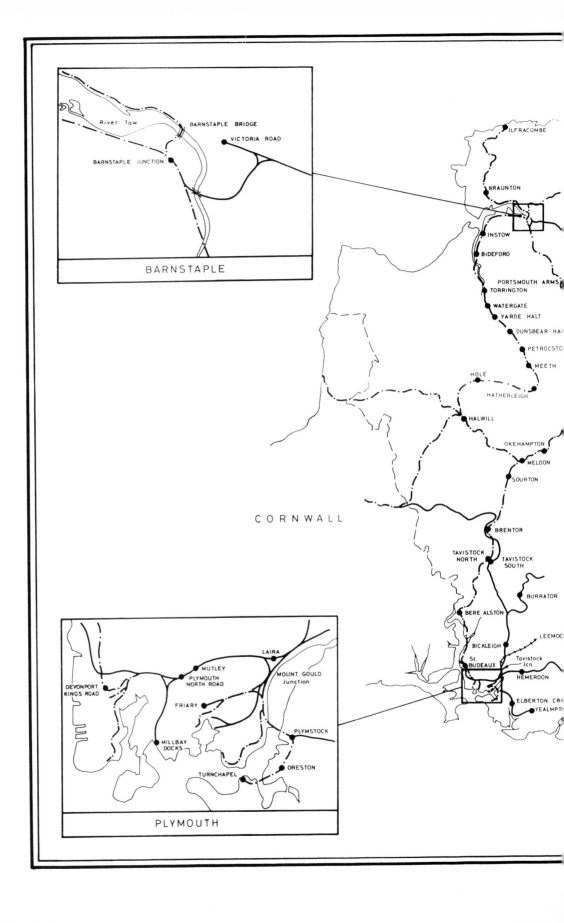

BARNSTAPLE

River Taw

BARNSTAPLE BRIDGE

VICTORIA ROAD

BARNSTAPLE JUNCTION

ILFRACOMBE

BRAUNTON

INSTOW

BIDEFORD

PORTSMOUTH ARMS
TORRINGTON

WATERGATE
YARDE HALT

DUNSBEAR HA

PETROCSTO

MEETH

HOLE

HATHERLEIGH

HALWILL

OKEHAMPTON

MELDON

SOURTON

CORNWALL

BRENTOR

TAVISTOCK
NORTH

TAVISTOCK
SOUTH

BURRATOR

BERE ALSTON

LEEMOC

BICKLEIGH

Tavistock
Jcn.

St.
BUDEAUX

HEMERDON

ELBERTON CR

YEALMPT

PLYMOUTH

LAIRA

MUTLEY

DEVONPORT
KINGS ROAD

PLYMOUTH
NORTH ROAD

MOUNT GOULD
Junction

FRIARY

MILLBAY
DOCKS

PLYMSTOCK

ORESTON

TURNCHAPEL

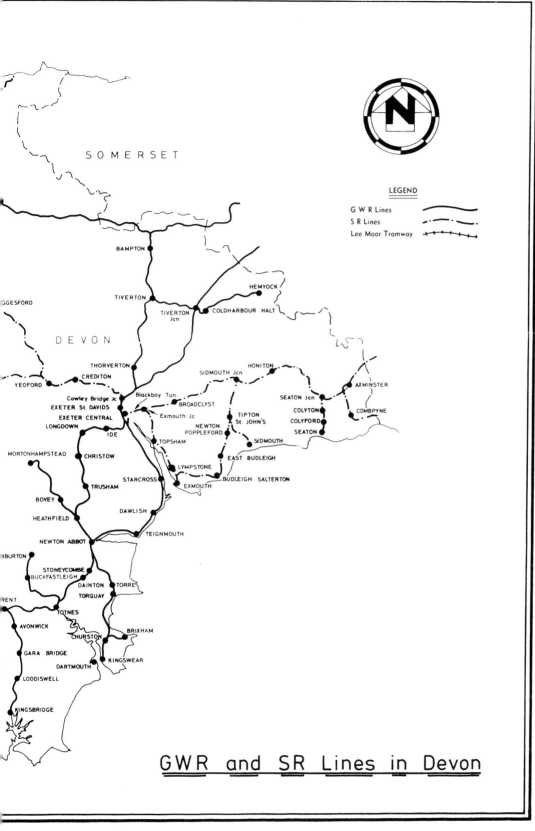

GWR and SR Lines in Devon

Reference Sources

The Locomotives of the Great Western Railway parts 2/3/5/8/9/10/12/13, The Railway Correspondence and Travel Society, 1952, 1956, 1958, 1968, 1962, 1966, 1974, 1983.

Locomotive Stock Book 1948/1950/1952/1960, The Railway Correspondence and Travel Society, 1948, 1950, 1952, 1960.

LSWR Locomotives. A survey. 1873–1922, F. Burtt, Ian Allen Ltd, 1950.

ABC British Railway Locomotives: Southern Region 1952, Ian Allen, 1952.

ABC Locoshed Book 1955, Ian Allen, 1955.

Track Layout Diagrams of the GWR and BRWR Sections 12/14/15, R.A. Cooke, 1984, 1985, 1986.

Track Layout Diagrams of the Southern Railway and BRSR Section 6, G.A. Pryer, R.A. Cooke, 1983.

British Railways Western Region working timetables, Plymouth/Exeter 1957/1958/1959/1960.

British Railways Southern Region (Western District), working timetables 1960.

Great Western Railway timetables, summer 1947.

British Railways Western Operating Area, service timetables, Plymouth District, summer 1951.

Southern Railway Passenger Services timetable, summer 1947.

The Plymouth Railway Circle magazine, various issues.

The Withered Arm (1967/8), T.W.E. Roche, Town and Country Press, 1967/8.

The Withered Arm (Railway World Special, 1988), Peter Semmens, Ian Allen, 1988.

An Historical Survey of Southern Sheds, Chris Hawkins and George Reeve, Oxford Publishing Company, 1979.

An Historical Survey of Great Western Engine sheds, 1947, E. Lyons, Oxford Publishing Company, 1972.

Sectional maps of the British Railways, Ian Allen, 1948.

The Ashburton Branch (and the Totnes Quay Line), Anthony R. Kingdom, Oxford Publishing Company, 1977.

The Newton Abbot to Kingswear Railway (1844–1988), C.R. Potts, Oakwood Press, 1991.

The Teign Valley Line, L.W. Pomroy, Oxford Publishing Company, 1984.

The Brixham Branch, C.R. Potts, Oakwood Press, 1986.

The North Devon and Cornwall Junction Light Railway, C.F.D. Whetmath and Douglas Stuckey, Oakwood Press, 1963.

A History of the Southern Railway, C.F. Dendy-Marshall, Southern Railway Company, 1936.

The Barnstaple and Ilfracombe Railway, C. Maggs, Oakwood Press, 1978/88.

Railways to Exmouth, C. Maggs, Oakwood Press, 1980.

The Sidmouth, Seaton and Lyme Regis Branches, C. Maggs and P. Paye, Oakwood Press, 1979.

A Regional History of the Railways of Great Britain, volume 1, The West Country, David St John Thomas, David and Charles, 1960, 1963, 1966, 1973, 1981.

GWR Locomotive Allocations, First and Last Sheds 1922–1967, J.W.P. Rowledge, David and Charles, 1986.

Industrial Locomotives of South Western England, Industrial Railway Society, Handbook H, Industrial Railway Society, 1977.

The Last Days of Steam in Plymouth and Cornwall, Maurice Dart, Alan Sutton Publishing Ltd, 1990.

My personal record books since 1947 of locomotive sightings, photography and locomotive allocations.

Swindon-built LMS 8F 2–8–0 48410 from St Phillip's Marsh shed (Bristol) takes a rake of empty coaching stock out of St Budeaux West 'Down' goods loop bound for Wearde sidings on 6.8.57; a remnant of the original Cornwall Railway route between Saltash and St Germans, which was retained until 2.12.64 as carriage sidings.

Mike Daly

'Britannia' class 4–6–2 70016 'Ariel' from Laira shed heads an 'Up' express past St Budeaux West, having just entered Devon by crossing the Royal Albert Bridge over the River Tamar in September 1952.

Mike Daly

'Hall' class 4–6–0 5975 'Winslow Hall' from Westbury shed halts at St Budeaux Ferry Road, with an excursion train for Dawlish Warren on 6.6.59.

Mike Daly

'Britannia' class 4–6–2 70015 'Apollo', an Old Oak Common engine, pilots an unidentified 'Hall' class 4–6–0 on the 'Up' 'Limited' through St Budeaux Ferry Road in the early fifties.

Mike Daly

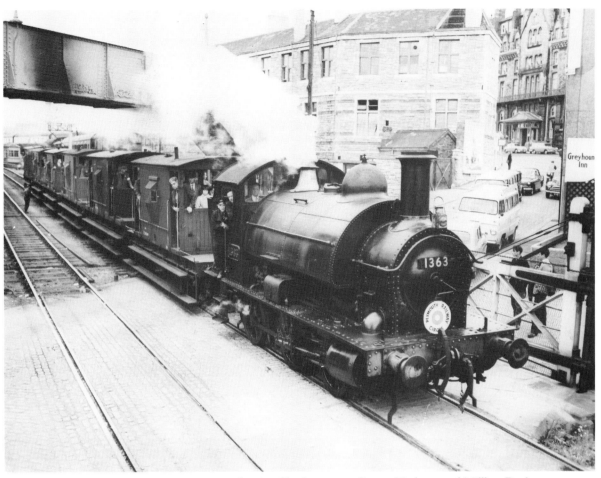

Plymouth Railway Circle ran a special train of brake vans to Sutton Harbour and Millbay Docks on 3.4.61. It is seen here at Millbay crossing hauled by 1361 class 0–6–0ST 1363, a Laira engine, descending the incline on a 1 in 51 gradient from Millbay station to the docks.

Western Morning News Newspapers Ltd

Millbay Docks with 1361 class 0–6–0ST 1363 (Laira) taking a train of wagons and vans in on 9.8.52 for off-loading on to ships. Note the passenger tenders for transferring passengers from liners, and the piles of timber.

Mike Daly

6400 class 0–6–0 PT 6430 of Laira shed waits at Plymouth (North Road) to depart with the 2.12 p.m. to Tavistock South on 14.7.62.

Maurice Dart

4575 class 2–6–2T 5557 from Laira shed with 'Castle' class 4–6–0 4083 'Abbotsbury Castle', a Penzance engine, at Plymouth North Road, await clearance to proceed to Laira MPD in the mid-fifties.

Mike Daly

Activity at the east end of Plymouth North Road on 3.8.57 with 4300 class 'Mogul' 7333 from Truro shed backing out past 'King' class 4–6–0 6028 'King George VI' and a 'Hall' class 4–6–0 with another 'Hall' shunting coaches beyond. 7333 was numbered 9311 until modified in June 1957.

Mike Daly

'Grange' class 4–6–0 6873 'Caradoc Grange' from Laira shed pilots a 'King' class 4–6–0 out of Plymouth North Road on the 'Up' 'Limited' in the mid-fifties. An SR 0–4–4T loco stands at platform 6 waiting to run to Friary shed.

Mike Daly

4700 class 2–8–0 4703 from Laira shed backs down to Plymouth North Road from Laira in the early fifties.

Mike Daly

'Modified Hall' class 4–6–0 6966 'Witchingham Hall' from Banbury shed blasts out of Plymouth North Road up the 1 in 55 bank to Mutley tunnel with an 'Up' milk train in the early fifties.

Mike Daly

Steam has been ousted from Plymouth. Diesel hydraulic D1027 'Western Lancer' from Laira depot climbs past the site of Mutley station on 16.6.64 with the 'Up' 'Limited' – a red liveried loco pulling chocolate and cream coaches.

Maurice Dart

'Castle' class 4–6–0 5021 'Whittington Castle', a Laira engine climbs out of Plymouth North Road past the site of Mutley station in the late fifties with the 'Royal Duchy' – the 11.00 a.m. Penzance–Paddington.

Mike Daly

'King' class 4–6–0 6013 'King Henry VIII' an Old Oak Common engine, passing Mutley on the way to Laira shed in the early fifties. The tunnel portal is now obscured by an overline car park.

Denis Richards

19

WD 2–8–0 90225 (ex-77310) from Ebbw Junction (Newport) shed at Laira, with a 2884 class 2–8–0 behind, in the shed yard sidings adjoining Laira marshalling yard.

Mike Daly

2800 class 2–8–0 2807 from Severn Tunnel Junction shed comes on to the coaling line at Laira on 14.5.60.

Maurice Dart

'King' class 4–6–0 6016 'King Edward V', an Old Oak Common engine backs out of Laira shed yard on 27.5.62. This engine will traverse 'The Speedway' curve, and reverse through Lipson Junction to reach Plymouth North Road tender first to attach to its train. The new diesel depot is visible behind the engine.

Maurice Dart

One of Laira's own 'Castle' class 4–6–0s 4087 'Cardigan Castle'. Constructed in June 1925 this loco was fitted with a double chimney and a four-row superheater in February 1958, and is seen at Laira in immaculate external condition on 18.2.62, being one of the 'Boat Engines' rostered to work 'Ocean Liner' specials from Millbay Docks to Paddington.

Maurice Dart

The coaling line at Laira shed on 8.7.62 with 'Castle' class 4–6–0 7012 'Barry Castle' (Stafford Road, Wolverhampton) leading a pair of 2884 class 2–8–0s, 3854 (St Phillip's Marsh, Bristol) and 3849 (Laira). Note the piles of ash from the smoke-boxes and clinker from the fire-boxes, with an oil can between the rails.

Maurice Dart

A trio of 'County' class 4–6–0s, all withdrawn in the yard at Laira where they were shedded, wait forlornly with their chimneys covered for their final journey to Swindon on 31.3.63. The locos are 1003 'County of Wilts', 1015 'County of Gloucester', and 1004 'County of Somerset'. All have had their smokebox and cabside number-plates and name-plates removed.

Maurice Dart

Laira shed yard in the early fifties. The visible engines are 'Castle' class 4–6–0 4088 'Dartmouth Castle' and 'Grange' class 4–6–0 6802 'Bampton Grange' – both Laira engines.

Mike Daly

A pair of Laira's stud of 4575 class 2–6–2Ts on 21.2.60. At their home shed are 5531 and 5569. The 'hoist' was removed and installed in the maintenance shed at the new Cardiff Canton diesel depot.

Maurice Dart

8750 class 0–6–0 PT 3686, a Laira engine, on shed pilot duty at its home shed 'sitting' astride the coaler incline on 22.11.59. I once observed this loco bringing a train of ninety-three empty wagons and vans into Laira goods yard on a 'transfer trip' from Tavistock Junction yard.

Maurice Dart

6400 class 0–6–0 PT 6408 (Laira) in the one road 'works' at Laira receiving attention to a 'hot box' on 21.2.60.

Maurice Dart

The last of Laira's 1361 class 0–6–0STs 1363 stands withdrawn from service in the shed yard at Laira on 31.3.63. This loco has been preserved, firstly at Bodmin General, and now at Didcot. Laira shed closed to steam in April 1964.

Maurice Dart

For a short while Newton Abbot shed gained three members of the large 7200 class 2–8–2Ts on its allocation. This is a rare and slightly damaged photograph, taken in August 1951, of 7200 itself, bearing an 'NA' shed stencil, in the yard at Laira shed.

Maurice Dart

The Plymouth Railway Circle Brake van special to Yealmpton on 27.2.60 at Elburton Cross in charge of 4500 class 2–6–2T 4549 (Laira), during a photographic stop. Most participants are warmly clothed to keep out the south-west wind and cold damp air.

Mike Daly

Yealmpton station on 27.2.60 with Laira 4500 class 2–6–2T 4549 about to run round the Plymouth Railway Circle Brake van special. The Yealmpton branch closed to all traffic on 29.2.60.

Mike Daly

'Modified Hall' class 4–6–0 7909 'Heveningham Hall' (Laira) pilots another 'Hall' class 4–6–0 past Tavistock Junction in the mid-fifties. The marshalling yard ('Up' and 'Down') is in the background with the branch line to Tavistock and Launceston diverging left.

Mike Daly

BR 4MT 4–6–0 75028 (Laira) pilots 'Britannia' class 4–6–2 70018 'Flying Dutchman' (Old Oak Common) on the 12 noon Penzance–Liverpool Lime Street, as it skirts the banks of the River Plym at Crabtree in 1954.

Mike Daly

4500 class 2–6–2T 4530 (Laira) brings a Launceston to Plymouth North Road (on to Millbay as ECS) (probably 2.05 p.m. ex-Launceston), over Lee Moor Crossing between Plym Bridge platform and Marsh Mills on 12.3.54. Notice the grass-covered track for the horse-drawn 4 ft 6 in gauge Lee Moor Tramway wagons, with a catch point to guard the crossing; rather less well known than its counterpart over the GWR main line at Laira Junction.

The late Roy Sambourne, Maurice Dart Collection

The final passenger working on the branch line to Tavistock and Launceston was the 6.20 p.m. from Plymouth North Road on 29.12.62 which, headed by 4575 class 2–6–2T 5568 (Laira), encountered blizzard conditions and finally reached Tavistock at 12.25 a.m. Sunday morning and was unable to either proceed or return owing to snowdrifts blocking the line at Mary Tavy and Grenofen tunnel. The train crew maintained steam until the water ran out, the supply on the station having frozen. It is seen here, still in steam at 6.45 a.m. on 30.12.62 with the snow-covered funeral wreath still in place having defied the elements. The author and the loco fireman firmly tied it on before leaving North Road station.

Maurice Dart

Tavistock South in the late fifties with Laira 4575 class 2–6–2T 5567 running in with a Launceston–Plymouth North Road (on to Millbay as ECS) working, while 4800 class 0–4–2T 1434 (Laira) takes water having worked in from North Road on an auto-working.

Mike Daly

4400 class 2–6–2T 4410 with a mixed train bound for Princetown climbing at 1 in 40 between Burrator Halt and Ingra Tor Halt in desolate country, typical of the line, with a strong wind blowing the steam well clear of the engine. These small-wheeled (4 ft 1½ in) Prairie tanks were the mainstay of the line for many years, with one being sub-shedded from Laira at the tiny shed at Princetown. The line closed on 5.3.56. Both the 9.04 a.m. and 2.51 p.m. trains from Yelverton to Princetown ran 'mixed'.

Maurice Dart Collection

'Grange' class 4–6–0 6801 'Aylburton Grange' (Penzance) pilots a 'King' class 4–6–0 past Tavistock Junction yards in the mid-fifties on an 'Up' express.

Mike Daly

4300 class 2–6–0 5327 from Swindon shed heads an 'Up' freight out of Tavistock Junction yards, while a 'banker' waits in the background to provide assistance on Hemerdon bank in the mid-fifties.

Mike Daly

St Blazey 4200 class 2–8–0T 4206 runs light engine on the 'Down' road, bunker first, to Tavistock Junction yards on 9.5.53.

Mike Daly

'Grange' class 4–6–0 6859 'Yiewsley Grange' from Cardiff (Canton) shed pilots a 'Hall' class 4–6–0 'Up' Hemerdon bank in the late fifties on the 'Up' 'Perishables', the 4.42 p.m. Plymouth North Road–Paddington.

Mike Daly

'Castle' class 4–6–0 5023 'Brecon Castle' from Laira shed storms up Hemerdon bank (1 in 42/1 in 41 for 2 ¼ miles) unassisted in the late fifties with an 'Up' passenger working.

Mike Daly

Brent station in June 1960 with a 'Down' express stopped to disembark passengers wishing to join the two-coach Kingsbridge branch train whose crew are sitting on the platform seat prior to climbing into 4575 class 2–6–2T 5558 to start the journey to the South Hams. The engine is sub-shedded at Kingsbridge. Brent station closed on 5.10.64.

Harry Cowan

3150 class 2–6–2T 3187 of Laira shed returning down the bank on 9.5.53 having assisted a freight on the climb to Hemerdon summit.

Mike Daly

4500 class 2–6–2T 4561 from Newton Abbot shed runs around the Kingsbridge branch train at Brent on 3.8.59.

Maurice Dart

4575 class 2–6–2T 5558 sub-shedded at Kingsbridge at Avonwick with a train for Brent in June 1959.

Harry Cowan

4575 class 2–6–2T 5533 from Kingsbridge shed leaves Gara Bridge where it has crossed another train, and proceeds over the level crossing bound for Brent in June 1959.

Harry Cowan

Loddiswell station with a train for Brent in charge of 4575 class 2–6–2T 5533, a Kingsbridge sub-shedded engine in June 1959. Note the camping coach in the siding.

Harry Cowan

Kingsbridge station with 4575 class 2–6–2T 5573 shedded on the branch, taking water prior to departing with a train for Brent and tackling the initial climb at 1 in 50 to Sorley tunnel on 29.8.59. On 16.9.63 the Kingsbridge branch closed completely.

Terry Nicholls

4500 class 2–6–2T 4561 from Newton Abbot shed awaits departure at Kingsbridge terminus in June 1959.

Harry Cowan

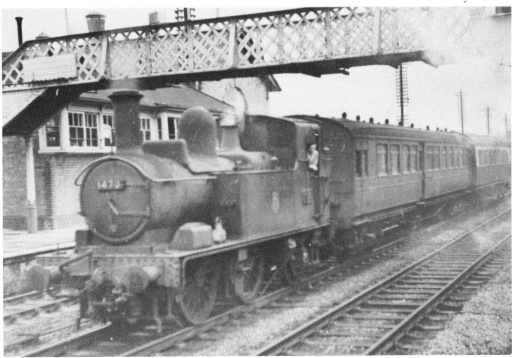

4800 class 0–4–2T 1470, sub-shedded at Ashburton, waits at Totnes on the 'Up' main line on 28.10.57 – out of the way of an 'Up' stopping train. It has two auto-coaches and will later propel them to Ashburton, departing at 4.55 p.m.

Maurice Dart

Plymouth Railway Circle ran a farewell train of brake vans to Ashburton on 8.9.62, hauled by 4500 class 2–6–2T 4567 of Laira shed which had actually been condemned within the previous two days; special permission was obtained to use it for this train, which also visited the Totnes Quay branch and is seen here at Totnes Town level crossing. The branch to Totnes Quay was officially taken out of use on 7.12.69.

Maurice Dart

4500 class 2–6–2T 4567 (Laira) stands at Buckfastleigh with the Plymouth Railway Circle's Ashburton special on 8.9.62. This site is now the headquarters of the Dart Valley Railway, the Ashburton branch having closed completely two days after this tour took place, but re-opened privately in April 1969 being truncated to Buckfastleigh from 3.10.71.

Maurice Dart

Dainton sidings are on the right as the 12.25 a.m. Manchester London Road–Penzance clears the tunnel and begins the descent to Totnes on 3.7.59 headed by 'Hall' class 4–6–0 4905 'Barton Hall' from Hereford shed piloted by 'Castle' class 4–6–0 4080 'Powderham Castle' from Bath Road (Bristol) shed.

Peter Gray

The 12.20 p.m. Penzance–Kensington milk train drifts down Dainton bank having just passed Stoneycombe on 11.7.58 hauled by 2800 class 2-8-0 2881 piloted by 'Castle' class 4–6–0 4098 'Kidwelly Castle' both from Newton Abbot shed.

Peter Gray

The Plymouth Railway Circle's farewell brake van trip enters Ashburton on 8.9.62 behind Laira's 4500 class 2–6–2T 4567. Note the loco shed behind the train.

The late Cedric Owen, Maurice Dart Collection

4800 class 0–4–2T 1427 (Newton Abbot) leaves Torre with the 10.50 a.m. auto-train to Moreton-hampstead on 10.5.58. Note a cafeteria car on the rear, probably being worked empty to Newton Abbot.

Peter Gray

A Penzance engine, 4500 class 2–6–2T 4566, leaves Torquay on 20.7.60 with the 8.10 p.m. Newton Abbot–Paignton. This was the last steam loco officially to be repaired at Newton Abbot factory, leaving there on 15.7.60 and still on running in turns.

Peter Gray

4800 class 0–4–2T 1470 shedded at Newton Abbot waits at Churston with the 12.35 p.m. auto-train
to Brixham on 3.8.59.

Maurice Dart

4800 class 0–4–2T 1427 from Newton Abbot shed stands at Brixham waiting to propel back down
the branch to Churston in June 1959. The Brixham branch closed completely on 13.5.63.

Harry Cowan

5101 class 2–6–2T 4150 from Newton Abbot shed skirts the River Dart approaching Britannia Halt (an unadvertised station) with the 4.33 p.m. Kingswear–Newton Abbot on 19.5.57. The photograph was taken from the Higher Ferry.

Maurice Dart

'Castle' class 4–6–0 5023 'Brecon Castle' from Laira shed, marshalling stock at Kingswear on 19.5.57. The BR service from Paignton to Kingswear officially ceased on 28.10.72, followed by a period of BR working for the Dart Valley Railway until a complete take over on 31.12.72.

Maurice Dart

On 19.5.57 4-4-0 *City of Truro* worked a special train to Kingswear. It returned to Newton Abbot shed for coal and water, then ran back to Kingswear where it used the turntable, instead of that at Newton Abbot. It is seen here just prior to backing on to the turntable.

Maurice Dart

4–4–0 *City of Truro* backs off the turntable at Kingswear on 19.5.57 prior to working its special train back up the line to Newton Abbot. A train has just arrived hauled by Newton Abbot 5101 class 2–6–2T 4178.

Maurice Dart

There was a GWR station at Dartmouth without any trains, which had a connecting ferry service across the River Dart to Kingswear station. The service was worked from 31.5.08 until 8.10.54 by 'The Mew', seen here just off the landing stage at Dartmouth.

Maurice Dart Collection

Newton Abbot West signal-box is behind 2884 2–8–0 2887 of Severn Tunnel Junction shed which is heading on 'Up' freight past the station on 14.6.61.

Peter Gray

At Newton Abbot on 30.4.62 'Modified Hall' class 4–6–0 7901 'Doddington Hall' from Bath Road (Bristol) shed is shunting departmental wagons and vans in the lower shed yard, while a 'Castle' class 4–6–0 and a class 22 diesel hydraulic stand outside the shed. In the sidings are a 5101 class 2–6–2T, a diesel multiple unit and a 350 hp diesel shunter.

Maurice Dart

A Cardiff Canton-allocated 2884 class 2–8–0 2889 brings a 'Down' freight through Newton Abbot on 7.5.60.

Maurice Dart

Newton Abbot station used to be the home for 'Tiny', a broad gauge South Devon Railway 0–4–0 vertical boiler loco built in January 1868 by Sara & Co. It worked on the Sutton Harbour branch at Plymouth replacing horses and after withdrawal in June 1883, it was used as a stationary boiler at Newton Abbot Factory until 1927. In April 1980 the loco was transferred to the Dart Valley Railway Museum at Buckfastleigh, and is seen at Newton Abbot on 13.5.56.

Maurice Dart

4–4–0 *City of Truro* approaches Newton Abbot with a special working to Kingswear on 19.5.57. Newton Abbot East signal-box is in the background.

Maurice Dart

BR 5MT 4–6–0 73133, a Shrewsbury engine, stands at the outlet from Newton Abbot shed yard which is full of locos in August 1958.

Mike Daly

The coaling line at Newton Abbot shed on 10.2.57 with three local engines. They are 5700 class 0–6–0PT 5796, 4500 class 2–6–2T 4568 and 'Grange' class 4–6–0 6829 'Burmington Grange'.

Maurice Dart

Newton Abbot shed yard on 13.5.56. The visible locos are BR 3MT 2–6–2Ts 82006 and 82033, both Newton engines, and a Truro engine ex-Newton Abbot Factory, 4500 class 2–6–2T 4561.

Maurice Dart

A trio of Laira engines outside Newton Abbot Factory on 13.5.56. These are 5101 class 2-6-2T 5175, 1361 class 0–6–0ST 1363 and 6400 class 0–6–0PT 6406.

Maurice Dart

On 6.6.60 the South Devon Railway Society ran a special train, 'The Heart of Devon Rambler' from Paignton to Moretonhampstead, hauled by 5101 class 2–6–2T 4174 from Newton Abbot shed. It is seen passing through Heathfield, junction for the Teign Valley line, some of the trains on which terminated here, in the bay platform occupied by wagons for Ball clay traffic from Teignbridge sidings. The siding going off to the right of the picture once served Candy & Co. Pottery Works.

Peter Gray

Taff Vale Railway 127 became GWR 361, this 0–6–2T being withdrawn in January 1957. After several months its boiler was sent to Newton Abbot for steam-generating duties at the loco factory, outside which it is seen on 23.11.57 awaiting installation within.

Maurice Dart

The signalman at Bovey (the station at Bovey Tracey) removes the 'token' for the last public passenger train on the branch, this being the 9.10 p.m. Moretonhampstead–Newton Abbot on 28.2.59.

Maurice Dart

On 7.6.58 4800 class 0–4–2T 1427 (Newton Abbot) has arrived at Moretonhampstead with the 2.15 p.m. auto-working from Newton Abbot and is running round the train to detach a van from the rear. Passenger services ceased on 28.2.59.

Peter Gray

On 4.3.61 the South Devon Railway Society ran a special train formed of brake vans over the Teign Valley line, hauled by Newton Abbot 5101 class 2–6–2T 4117. It is seen running round the train at Trusham, the limit of working. The Teign Valley line was closed to passengers on 9.6.58 and completely closed beyond Christow on the same date. Ashton and Christow closed on 1.5.61 following flooding which washed away a section of track and Trusham was closed on 5.4.65, leaving Heathfield and Chudleigh which closed on 4.12.67.

Maurice Dart Collection

Christow station was a crossing place on the Teign Valley line. On 19.1.58 at 1.20 p.m. the 12.45 p.m. Exeter St David's to Newton Abbot in charge of 5700 class 0–6–0PT 7761 runs into Christow where 4800 class 0–4–2T 1469 waits, with the 12.40 p.m. Newton–Exeter. Both engines are shedded at Exeter.

Peter Gray

4575 class 2–6–2T 5558 from Newton Abbot shed working a Teign Valley train from Heathfield is about to enter the 248 yard Culver tunnel leading to Longdown station on 7.6.58.
Maurice Dart Collection

During June 1958 an Exeter engine, 4575 class 2–6–2T 5536, brings a Heathfield to Exeter St David's train into Longdown station, which, apart from being a very hilly mile from the village it purported to serve, was sandwiched between two tunnels, Culver (248 yd) and Perridge (836 yd), both used for growing mushrooms since closure.

Harry Cowan

Exeter-based 4800 class 0–4–2T 1451 brings a Teign Valley train bound for Exeter St David's into Ide Halt.

The late Arthur Luxton, Maurice Dart Collection

Sunday single-line working was in operation when this photograph was taken of 'Castle' class 4–6–0 5021 'Whittington Castle' from Laira shed crossing back on to the 'Down' line at Teignmouth on 21.6.59 with the 10.40 a.m. Paddington–Falmouth. On 1.4.68 the 'Up' goods sidings curving in left were taken out of use.

Mike Daly

'Hall' class 4–6–0 4992 'Crosby Hall' from Laira shed brings a 'Down' freight out of Parsons tunnel (513 yd) and on to the sea wall between Dawlish and Teignmouth at 4 p.m. on 10.8.54.

Maurice Dart Collection

Class 22 diesel hydraulic D6316 from Laira depot pilots 'Castle' class 4–6–0 7033 'Hartlebury Castle' from Old Oak Common shed past Dawlish with a 'Down' express on 14.8.61.

Larry Crosier

A BR 9F 2–10–0 brings a 'Down' freight through Dawlish towards the 205-yd Kennaway tunnel which together with the four other tunnels through the cliffs will provide temporary respite for the train from the battering of the stormy sea captured in this rare photograph.

Maurice Dart Collection

'King' class 4–6–0 6021 'King Richard II' approaches Starcross with the Sunday 10.40 a.m. Paddington–Falmouth express on 19.7.59. The loco was shedded at Laira at this time.

Peter Gray

A Laira engine, 2884 class 2–8–0 3863 blankets Exeter St David's with steam as it accelerates a 'Down' freight through the station past a diesel multiple unit on 10.2.62.

Mike Daly

A snowy night at Exeter St David's. It is 11.00 p.m. on 19.1.63 as St Phillip's Marsh-allocated 'Hall' class 4–6–0 4992 'Crosby Hall' stands on the centre road with a 'Down' freight.

Alistair Jeffery

Exeter-based 5101 class 2–6–2T 4174 awaits the 'right-away' at Exeter St David's on 10.2.57 with a stopping train for Kingswear. These locos performed well on such services, possessing excellent acceleration and a good turn of speed.

Maurice Dart

At 10.10 p.m. at Exeter St Davids on 7.7.58 the last public Teign Valley passenger train is waiting to leave in charge of Newton Abbot's 4575 class 2–6–2T 5533, carrying flowers and wreaths laid above the buffers just in front of the smokebox. The train was timed to depart at 9.30 p.m. and had been delayed by 'funeral rites' on the Teign Valley line, more of which took place on its journey back along that line to Newton Abbot.

Maurice Dart

On 16.9.61 the station pilot at Exeter St David's was locally-shedded 5400 class 0–6–0 PT 5412, an engine which spent many years at Laira shed, being a favourite for the Yealmpton branch auto-train.

Maurice Dart

Exeter St David's on 3.11.62 with 4800 class 0–4–2T 1471 (Exeter) in platform 1 on the 8.15 p.m. Exe Valley working to Tiverton.

Alistair Jeffery

Exeter shed with a very rare visiting loco in the form of 2884 class 2–8–0 3828 from Croes Newydd shed (Wrexham) on 22.3.59.

Maurice Dart

4800 class 0–4–2T 1462 leaves Tiverton on 18.4.60 with the 12.25 p.m. auto-train to Tiverton Junction where this loco was sub-shedded from Exeter. Passenger services ceased on 5.10.64 with freight ending on 5.6.67.

Maurice Dart

Exeter shed on 11.10.59 with the autumn afternoon sun throwing a shadow of 4800 class 0–4–2T 1462 on to the side of 4575 class 2–6–2T 5524. Both locos are shedded at Exeter.

Maurice Dart

A West Country loco for many years was 2021 class 0–6–0 PT 2088 seen here at Exeter on shed pilot duty in the early fifties. Built at Wolverhampton Stafford Road Works in March 1901 it survived until August 1955, ending its days at Taunton shed.

Maurice Dart Collection

Exeter shed yard seen from the platform at St David's on 16.9.61. Lined up with their chimneys 'capped' are stored 4800 class 0–4–2Ts 1420, 1471 and 1434, all local engines, having been displaced by diesel multiple units or class 22 diesel hydraulic locos.

Maurice Dart

After closure in October 1963 Exeter shed remained empty for some months and roofless, but with the displacement of steam locos at Taunton and Exmouth Junctions by diesels, it was used to store withdrawn locos. Here on 26.6.64 are 2251 class 0–6–0s 3205 and 2214 with an SR N class 2–6–0 31842.

Maurice Dart

Stored at Exeter GWR shed on 26.6.64 is withdrawn SR N class 2–6–0 31821, previously shedded at Exmouth Junction.

Maurice Dart

2251 class 0–6–0 3205 shedded at Exmouth Junction worked the RCTS/PRC special 'The Exmoor Ranger' on its final leg from Ilfracombe to Exeter St David's via Taunton, on 27.3.65. It is seen at Cowley Bridge Junction, north-east of Exeter St David's, with the SR route to North Devon, North Cornwall and Plymouth diverging left behind the signal-box.

The late Cedric Owen, Maurice Dart Collection

'County' class 4–6–0 1023 'County of Oxford' shedded at Laira, races through Tiverton Junction with an 'Up' Bank Holiday relief on 18.4.60. Branch lines to Tiverton and Hemyock diverged here.

Maurice Dart

4800 class 0–4–2T 1451 waits in the early sixties while the crossing gates are opened to permit access to Coldharbour Halt with a train from Hemyock to Tiverton Junction where the branch engine was sub-shedded.

John Gronwalt Collection

4800 class 0–4–2T 1440 stands at Hemyock station waiting to return with the 3 p.m. to Tiverton Junction on 18.4.60. The coach is gas-lit ex-Barry Railway W263W, which together with a similar vehicle W268W, formed the coaching stock for the branch. The line was opened as a light railway on 29.5.1876 and closed to passengers on 9.9.63, milk traffic ceasing in October 1975. Two sidings once continued over separate level crossings to serve the milk factory.

Maurice Dart

An Exeter engine, 4800 class 0–4–2T 1420 halts at Thorverton with the 7.40 p.m. Exeter St David's–Dulverton on 18.4.60. The Exe Valley closed to passengers on 7.10.63 with grain traffic to Thorverton lasting another year.

Maurice Dart

8750 class 0–6–0 PT 9629 from Exeter shed departs from Tiverton with the 11.45 a.m. Exeter St David's–Dulverton service on 18.4.60.

Maurice Dart

An Exeter engine, 4800 class 0–4–2T 1451, awaits departure from Bampton (Devon) with an Exeter St David's to Dulverton working. Note the goods shed beyond the station.

Maurice Dart Collection

Plymouth Railway Circle's farewell brake van trip to Yealmpton on 27.2.60 started from Plymouth Friary where 4500 class 2–6–2T 4549 from Laira shed is standing awaiting departure. Constructed in January 1915, this loco retained inside steam pipes until withdrawn in December 1961. Plymouth Friary opened on 1.7.1891. It was closed to passengers from 15.9.58 since when it has served as a goods station, then as a marshalling yard and latterly as a parcels depot, with the track layout becoming gradually more truncated, leaving only one line passing through the bridge to the platform.

Maurice Dart

Ex-Plymouth, Devonport and South Western Junction Railway 0–6–2T 30758 'Lord St Levan' shunts vans and open wagons towards the road bridge across Friary yard, *c.* 1955. This loco was shedded at Friary for most of its life, together with 30757, 'Earl of Mount Edgcumbe', with one usually being sub-shedded at Callington.

Mike Daly

02 class 0–4–4T 30183 from Friary shed shunts in Friary yard with a Plymouth Docks West Wharf match truck in the mid-fifties.

Denis Richards

G6 0–6–0T 30162 transferred to Friary shed from Eastleigh for a period is shunting Friary yard on 7.6.57.

Mike Daly

A 'double header' swings around Lipson No. 1 curve in the fifties past Laira shed which is full of locos, with a 'Grange' class 4–6–0 awaiting exit from 'The Speedway' curve. The train is heading for Mount Gould Junction and Friary headed by an N class 2–6–0 piloting 'West Country' class 4–6–2 34106 'Lydford' running tender first. Both locos were shedded at Exmouth junction.

Mike Daly

One of Friary shed's stud of B4 0–4–0Ts 30089 on the coaling line at its home shed in August 1957.
This loco was named 'Trouville' for many years, and still bore the name painted on its tanks when
transferred to Friary from Southampton Docks.

Denis Richards

Friary shed's B4 class 0–4–0T 30102 brings a train from the Cattewater branch past Lucas Terrace Halt, heading for Friary yard in July 1957. These engines were known at Friary shed as 'Bugs'.
Denis Richards

B4 class 0–4–0T 30102 pushing loaded wagons up the coal stage incline at its home shed Friary, where it was performing shed pilot duties in July 1957. When transferred from Southampton Docks to Friary this loco still carried the name 'Granville' painted on its tanks.

Denis Richards

On 30.9.61 Plymouth Railway Circle ran a farewell brake van tour to Turnchapel headed by a Friary engine, M7 class 0–4–4T 30034 seen at Oreston on the outward journey during a photographic stop.

Mike Daly

M7 class 0–4–4T 30034 of Friary shed prepares to run round at Turnchapel, having worked the Plymouth Railway Circle's farewell brake van trip. The line continued beyond the station through a short tunnel to the Admiralty pier and wharf. Closure to passengers was from 10.9.51 and to goods traffic beyond Plymstock from 30.9.61, the date on which the special train ran.

Maurice Dart

Mount Gould Junction with Friary shed's G6 0–6–0T 30162 heading bunker first up the spur to Cattewater Junction, *c.* 1957. This line was the GWR No. 2 curve used by the service from Millbay to Yealmpton between 1898 and 1930. It was closed to all traffic on 15.9.58 and the track removed on 27.9.58 the same year. The lines at bottom left run to Friary Junction with the track of the Lee Moor Tramway parallelling them on the right. In the distance the left-hand line is the No. 1 curve to Lipson Junction while that curving right runs to Laira yard, nowadays the site of Laira traction maintenance depot and carriage sidings. Mount Gould and Tothill Halt, which was only open for twelve and a quarter years, was on the No. 2 curve and the loco will shortly pass the site.

Mike Daly

It is 13.6.64 and the 'West Country' class 'Pacifics' and N class 'Moguls' have been displaced by diesel hydraulics on the SR line to Plymouth. 'Hymek' D7068, based at Newton Abbot, passes through Mutley with empty stock from the 8.42 a.m. Exeter Central–Plymouth which it is taking into Friary.

Maurice Dart

Plymouth (North Road) with rebuilt 'West Country' class 'Pacific' 34098 'Templecombe' shedded at Exmouth Junction waiting to depart with the 7.21 p.m. to Exeter Central on 5.8.61.

Maurice Dart

A rare visitor to the Plymouth area outside Devonport King's Road, a station which seems to have been rarely photographed. 0395 class 0–6–0 30564 (originally SR 3029) from Exmouth Junction shed has deposited a freight train in the spacious goods yard, *c.* 1955, and has regained the 'Down' main line to run to Friary shed for servicing and turning. This engine was one of the Adams 496 class built in 1886 with long front overhang and was later fitted with a Drummond boiler, being withdrawn during 1958. Like Friary, the yard at Devonport was crossed by a long road bridge visible behind the engine but also other bridges near its throat. The goods depot is visible top right, while behind the signal-box, visible through the bridge, an incline descended via a 50-yd-long curved tunnel to run to Stonehouse Pool. Until 2.6.1890, Devonport was the LSWR terminus and the 'Up' and 'Down' lines were reversed, as trains approached from the North Road direction via Devonport Junction. The section from Devonport Junction to St Budeaux Victoria Road was closed to passengers on 7.9.64 and to all traffic beyond Devonport. Freight traffic here ceased on 7.3.71.

Mike Daly

A 'West Country' class 4–6–2, probably 34001 'Exeter', an Exmouth Junction engine, on the 'Up' 'City of Exeter Holiday Express' approaches St Budeaux Victoria Road on 5.8.57. The 'Holiday Expresses' were usually worked by a loco named after their starting point. St Budeaux East signalbox is on the right. The cutting through which the train has passed has been filled in and the bridge and embankment demolished.

Mike Daly

T9 class 4–4–0 30711 shedded at Exmouth Junction runs past St Budeaux SR goods yard and sidings with a stopping train to Exeter on 18.5.56. This area is now occupied by a lorry park, petrol station and taxi office.

Mike Daly

Exmouth Junction N class 2–6–0 31845 leaves St Budeaux Victoria Road past the replacement signal-box for the structure which was bombed, heading for Plymouth in the mid-fifties with a 'Down' passenger working.
Mike Daly

BR 4MT 4–6–0 75025, shedded at Laira, leaves St Budeaux Victoria Road in the mid-fifties with the 2.35 p.m. Plymouth North Road–Exeter Central – a train worked by a Western Region loco and crew to provide knowledge of the SR route in case of emergencies requiring diversions.
Mike Daly

LMS Fairburn 4MT 2–6–4T 42102 north of St Budeaux Victoria Road with a 'Down' train for Friary in November 1951. This engine was at the time, together with 42098 and 42103, allocated to Friary shed for about a month for trials as possible replacements for the T9 class 4–4–0s.

Mike Daly

Exmouth Junction-allocated 3MT 2–6–2T 82017 approaches St Budeaux Victoria Road with a train bound for Friary in late 1952.

Mike Daly

It has always been the case that one could never predict what might turn up on the railway. A most unusual sighting was Western Region departmental shunter PWM 650 passing along the SR north of St Budeaux Victoria Road in a Permanent Way train containing a WR brake van with a 'West Country' class 4–6–2 at each end, *c.* 1954.

Mike Daly

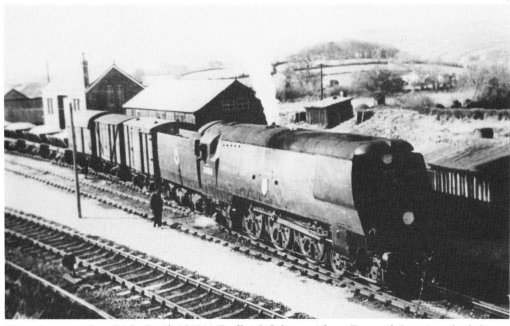

'West Country' class 'Light Pacific' 34014 'Budleigh Salterton' from Exmouth Junction shed shunts a train in Bere Alston goods yard on an unknown date. The train is probably the 8.20 a.m. Friary–Exmouth Junction.

Lens of Sutton

After the blizzard of 29.12.62 the SR had three engines in a snowdrift at Sourton Cutting near Bridestowe. They sent a train out from Friary to try to reach these engines and it stopped on the viaduct outside Tavistock North, hauled by 'Battle of Britain' class 4–6–2 34063 '229 Squadron', an Exmouth Junction engine. Tavistock station was blocked by snow and the train was unable to proceed until railwaymen aided by railway enthusiasts stranded on the previous night's 6.20 p.m. Plymouth–Launceston, had cleared the tracks between the platforms. Nearly two hours after arriving, the loco ran around and took everyone back to Devonport, having abandoned the idea of attempting to reach Sourton. This photograph was taken at 10.45 a.m. on 30.12.62.

Maurice Dart

Brentor station in the late fifties with an M7 0–4–4T from Friary shed on a three-coach train having run round. The train is the 4.14 p.m. from Plymouth (North Road) (4 p.m. ex-Friary ECS), which terminated here at 5.22 p.m. and is about to be propelled out, to come into the 'Down' platform via the crossover, departing again at 5.31 p.m. to Plymouth. Bere Alston to Lydford was closed to freight on 28.2.66 with the passenger service north of Bere Alston to Okehampton ending on 6.5.68. The loco is 30037; the photograph was taken on 28.8.56.

Lens of Sutton, The late Peter Tunks's Collection

Sourton Cutting north of Bridestowe in January 1963 with railwaymen attempting to dig N class 2–6–0 31838 from Exmouth Junction shed out of the snow, following the blizzard during the night of 29.12.62, with another loco visible in the background. A total of six locos became stranded here in a few days, as attempts to reach those already snowed up failed. The last three to be released were frozen so hard that it was necessary to ram them several times with a pair of locos to move them. They were rescued some three to four weeks after the blizzard. The line here skirted Dartmoor at 950 ft above sea level.

Western Morning News Newspapers Ltd

Meldon viaduct spans the valley of the West Okement River at a height of 120 ft. Consisting of six spans it was opened on 12.10.1874 and doubled on 22.12.1879 by constructing a second viaduct intertwined with the first. The 'Up' line over the viaduct was closed on 24.4.66 and the 'Down' line, which had been retained as a shunting neck for the quarry, closed on 6.5.68.

Maurice Dart Collection

Meldon Quarry loco shed on 31.12.61 containing G6 0–6–0T DS682 (ex-30238). The quarry supplied the SR with ballast and also small aggregate used to manufacture the pre-cast concrete structures which were a feature of SR routes.

Maurice Dart

'West Country' class 4–6–2 34007 'Wadebridge', an Exmouth Junction engine, rolls a loaded train
of ballast down the 1 in 77 bank from Meldon Quarry to Okehampton on 28.3.65.

Michael Messenger

Meldon Quarry on 18.10.66 with USA 0–6–0T DS234 (ex-30062) standing behind the small platform used by railwaymen, quarrymen and at one time quarrymen's wives, who were picked up here by a train from North Cornwall and taken to Okehampton on Saturdays to carry out the week's family shopping. This was the last BR steam loco working west of Bristol and Salisbury.

Maurice Dart

T9 class 4–4–0 30717, sub-shedded at Okehampton, shunts the 'Down' goods sidings north of the station in the mid-fifties, shrouding everywhere in steam, on a typically wet day.

Mike Daly

Okehampton shed on 26.11.55 with T9 class 4–4–0 30710, which was sub-shedded there, standing outside in the Dartmoor mist and rain.

Maurice Dart

Sub-shedded at Okehampton, N class 'Woolworth' 2–6–0 31831 stands inside the single road building on 6.12.59. The roofless shed affords little protection from the relentless Dartmoor rain as the shed floor shows.

Maurice Dart

Okehampton-based T9 class 4–4–0 30710 partly outside its home shed on 8.2.59 with the strong Dartmoor wind blowing steam well clear of the engine.

Maurice Dart

BR 3MT 2–6–2T 82011 sub-shedded at Bude runs round the train it has brought up to Halwill, ready to return, on 26.11.55. Services to Bude and Wadebridge ceased on 3.10.66.

Maurice Dart

On 27.4.63 Plymouth Railway Circle and the RCTS ran 'The North Cornishman' special from Exeter Central to Padstow. Hauled throughout by T9 class 4–4–0 120, repainted for preservation, it is at Halwill, one of several stops for operational and photographic requirements. On the return run between Okehampton and Cowley Bridge Junction, the engine certainly lived up to the type's nickname 'Greyhound' – reaching almost 90 mph.

Maurice Dart

Hole on 3.6.63 with LMS 2 MT 2–6–2T 41313 shedded at Barnstaple Junction on the 4 p.m. Torrington–Halwill. Note the vans in the goods yard.

Maurice Dart

LMS 2MT 2–6–2T 41313 from Barnstaple Junction shed at Hatherleigh on 3.6.63 with the 4 p.m. Torrington–Halwill.

Maurice Dart

Meeth on 3.6.63 with the 4 p.m. Torrington–Halwill in charge of LMS 2MT 2–6–2T 41313, a Barnstaple Junction engine.

Maurice Dart

LMS 2MT 2–6–2T 41313 from Barnstaple Junction shed on the 4 p.m. Torrington–Halwill at Petrockstow on 3.6.63. Passenger services on this line ceased on 1.3.65 with freight between Meeth and Barnstaple ending on 31.8.82.

Maurice Dart

LMS 2MT 2–6–2T 41313, a Barnstaple Junction engine, at Yarde Halt on 3.6.63 with the 4 p.m. Torrington–Halwill, in the rain.

Maurice Dart

Bideford station in June 1960 with M7 class 0–4–4T 30253, a Barnstaple Junction engine, waiting
clearance to proceed towards Torrington.

Harry Cowan

Torrington shed's allocation, an M7 class 0–4–4T, in the mid-fifties at one period was 30254, seen outside the tiny shed.

Terry Nicholls

'West Country' class 4–6–2 34030 'Watersmeet' enters Instow during a morning in June 1960 with empty stock to Torrington. This will return later and link up with an Ilfracombe portion at Barnstaple Junction to form a through train to Exeter Central and Waterloo. The engine is shedded at Exmouth Junction.

Harry Cowan

Entering Barnstaple Junction with a train from Ilfracombe on 23.4.62 is 'West Country' class 4–6–2 34015 'Exmouth' shedded at Exmouth Junction. The lines on the left ran to Bideford and Torrington.

Terry Nicholls

Barnstaple Junction on 25.8.62 with Exmouth Junction N class 2–6–0 31842 departing on a through working from Ilfracombe to Waterloo.

Michael Messenger

Activity at Barnstaple Junction on 23.4.62. GWR 4300 class 'Mogul' 6390 from Taunton shed waits on the centre road to back out and run into the shed yard, while 'Battle of Britain' class 4–6–2 34083 '605 Squadron' from Exmouth Junction shed runs in with a Waterloo to Ilfracombe service.

Terry Nicholls

Three Barnstaple Junction engines in the coaling area of the shed yard on 21.6.58. They are M7 class 0–4–4T 30256 and a pair of LMS 2MT 2–6–2Ts, one of which is 41295.

Maurice Dart

On 3.6.63 Barnstaple Junction shed had a very dilapidated look about it. Some of the locos visible are LMS 2MT 2–6–2Ts, 41298, 41310 and 41216, all shedded there, GWR 4300 class 2–6–0 7326 (ex-9304) shedded at Taunton, and SR N class 2–6–0 31818 shedded at Exmouth Junction.

Maurice Dart

Waiting in the yard at Barnstaple Junction shed, by this time merely a stabling and signing on point, is 2251 class 0–6–0 3205 from Exmouth Junction. It is 27.3.65 and the loco is ready to take over 'The Exmoor Ranger' special,which it will shortly follow to Ilfracombe, prior to working it back to Taunton and Exeter.

Maurice Dart

2251 class 0–6–0 3205 from Exmouth Junction shed heads 'The Exmoor Ranger' across Barnstaple bridge towards Barnstaple Junction on 27.3.65.

Michael Messenger

'Battle of Britain' class 4–6–2 34083 '605 Squadron', an Exmouth Junction engine, heads across the river bridge to Barnstaple Town with a Waterloo to Ilfracombe service on 23.4.62.

Terry Nicholls

Braunton station with 'The Exmoor Ranger' headed by a pair of Exmouth Junction LMS 2MT 2–6–2Ts, 41291 and 41206. The engines are taking water prior to tackling the 1 in 40 south side of Mortehoe bank on 27.3.65. This section closed to passengers on 5.10.70.

Michael Messenger

An Exmouth Junction engine, N class 2–6–0 31839, heads for the curve to the Taw River Bridge with a train from Barnstaple Junction to Ilfracombe on 21.4.62.

Terry Nicholls

LMS 2MT 2–6–2Ts 41291 and 41206 (both Exmouth Junction) attack the 1 in 40 bank from Braunton to Mortehoe and Woolacombe working 'The Exmoor Ranger' from Barnstaple Junction to Ilfracombe on 27.3.65.

Maurice Dart Collection

'Battle of Britain' class 4–6–2 34080 '74 Squadron' from Exmouth Junction shed drifts down the 1 in 36 bank past the reservoirs with the three-coach portion of the 'Atlantic Coast Express' for Ilfracombe on 13.9.63.

John Scrace, the late Peter Tunks's Collection

Ilfracombe station in the early fifties with a pair of N class 2–6–0s from Exmouth Junction shed, 31838 and 31845 awaiting their departures.

The late Peter Tunks's Collection

During its tour around North Devon on 27.3.65, 'The Exmoor Ranger' visited the GWR terminus at Barnstaple, Victoria Road, where LMS 2MT 2–6–2Ts 41291 and 41206, both Exmouth Junction shedded, are running round the train. Victoria Road closed to passengers on 13.6.60 and completely from 5.3.70.

Maurice Dart

On its way from Exeter to Barnstaple Junction, 'Battle of Britain' class 4–6–2 34081 '92 Squadron', shedded at Exmouth Junction, crossed an 'Up' passenger working at Portsmouth Arms on 21.4.62.
Terry Nicholls

After assisting 'The Exmoor Ranger' up Mortehoe bank, on 27.3.65, LMS 2MT 2–6–2Ts 41206 and 41291 stop at Eggesford, returning 'light engines' from Barnstaple Junction to Exmouth Junction, where they are shedded.

Maurice Dart Collection

N class 2–6–0 31847 from Exmouth Junction shed brings a freight from Plymouth Friary through Yeoford in the mid-fifties.

The late Peter Tunks's Collection

'Battle of Britain' class 4–6–2 34109 'Sir Trafford Leigh-Mallory' shedded at Exmouth Junction brings a 'Down' Plymouth service through Crediton in the late fifties.

The late Peter Tunks's Collection

'Battle of Britain' class 4–6–2 34080 '74 Squardron' from Exmouth Junction shed heads east on 14.4.62 from Exeter St Davids and approaches Cowley Bridge Junction where it will leave the GWR main line and head for Ilfracombe via Yeoford.

Terry Nicholls

N class 2–6–0 31836 from Exmouth Junction shed enters Exeter St David's on 10.2.57 with a train for Plymouth Friary, having just descended the 1 in 37 bank from Exeter Central. The GWR line to Newton Abbot goes straight ahead.

Maurice Dart

E1/R class 0–6–2T 32135 shedded at Exmouth Junction banks a freight hauled by an N class 2–6–0 out of Exeter St David's up the 1 in 37 incline to Exeter Central in the mid-fifties.

Mike Daly

On 30.4.62 Z class 0–8–0T 30955 from Exmouth Junction shed approaches a train stopped at Exeter St David's which it will assist up the incline to Exeter Central. The Zs were replaced by W 2–6–4Ts having themselves succeeded the E1/Rs. The Ws were replaced by 8750 class pannier tanks.

Maurice Dart

The downside yard at the south end of Exeter Central on 11.8.52 with 1750 hp Diesel electric 10202, which has just come off a train from Waterloo, a duty for which two of these locos were rostered for several years in the early fifties, this being an early attempt at replacing 'Merchant Navy' 'Pacifics' with diesel power.

Mike Daly

'West Country' class 4–6–2 34024 'Tamar Valley' shedded at Exmouth Junction brings a train from the Barnstaple line into Exeter St David's on 22.3.59.
Maurice Dart

On 23.3.66 LNER A4 class 4–6–2 60024 'Kingfisher' worked a special train from Exeter St David's to Waterloo. It has just reached the top of the incline, ¾ mile at 1 in 37 to enter Exeter Central.
Maurice Dart

Exeter Central during the afternoon of 5.10.57. E1/R class 0–6–2T 32697 and M7 class 0–4–4T 30374 are both marshalling coaching stock on the centre roads as T9 class 4–4–0 30715 starts away with a train for Plymouth Friary. All the locos are from Exmouth Junction shed.

Maurice Dart

N15 'King Arthur' class 4–6–0 30454 'Queen Guinevere' at Exeter Central on 5.10.57 with a train for Salisbury, where the loco is shedded.

Maurice Dart

An Exmouth Junction rebuilt 'Merchant Navy' class 4–6–2 35007 'Aberdeen Commonwealth' waits on the centre road at Exeter Central to attach the Exeter portion to an express for Waterloo on 22.6.58.

Maurice Dart

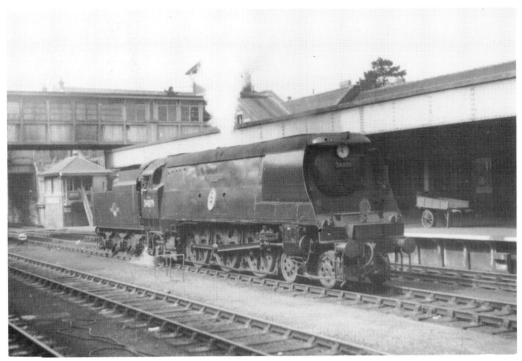

A 'Battle of Britain' class 4–6–2 from Exmouth Junction shed, 34079 '141 Squadron', waits on the centre road of a deserted Exeter Central on 7.4.63.

Maurice Dart

A 'Merchant Navy' class 4–6–2 35012 'United States Line' from Nine Elms shed awaits departure from Exeter Central with an express for Waterloo in the early fifties.

Mike Daly

On 11.8.52 S15 class 4–6–0 30841 from Exmouth Junction shed, heads a stopping train to Salisbury
out of Exeter Central past the 'A' signal-box.

Mike Daly

'Merchant Navy' class 4–6–2 35001 'Channel Packet' takes the 'Devon Belle' Pullman from Ilfracombe out of Exeter Central on 5.9.53 as M7 class 0–4–4T 30374 stands on the 'Down' road; both engines are shedded at Exmouth Junction.

Mike Daly

BR 4MT 2–6–4T 80039 from Exmouth Junction shed shunts in the 'Up-side' sidings at Exeter Central on 7.4.63.

Maurice Dart

BR 3MT 2–6–2T 82011 with a train for Exmouth has left Blackboy tunnel and approaches Exmouth Junction, where the loco is shedded, on 13.6.53.

Mike Daly

Exmouth Junction was the largest SR locomotive shed in the West Country, with an allocation, in 1952, of 144 and at one time it possessed seven sub-sheds. It closed to steam during 1965 and completely in March 1967, subsequently being demolished. Visible in the shed yard on 4.4.58 are an S15 class 4–6–0, and a trio of Bulleid 'Light Pacifics' (two 'West Countrys' and a 'Battle of Britain'), the locos being 30829 (Salisbury shed), 34106 'Lydford' (Exmouth Junction shed), 34035 'Shaftsbury' (Friary shed) and 34074 '46 Squadron' (Exmouth Junction shed).

Denis Richards

'Merchant Navy' class 4–6–2 35001 'Channel Packet' awaiting attention at Exmouth Junction, its home shed, on 14.5.51.

Maurice Dart

One of Exmouth Junction shed's rebuilt 'Merchant Navy' class 4–6–2s 35026 'Lamport and Holt Line' stands outside the shed on 7.4.63, with a line of withdrawn engines in the background.
Maurice Dart

An engine from Salisbury shed, H15 class 4–6–0 30333, stands alongside the shed at Exmouth Junction as a Bulleid 'Light Pacific' moves off to the front after taking on supplies of coal and water on 4.4.58.

Maurice Dart

An S15 class 4–6–0 from Salisbury shed, 30829, stands on the 'Ash Road' at Exmouth Junction on 22.12.63. This class were employed on milk trains to Exeter at the time.

Maurice Dart

BR 4MT 4–6–0 75025 outside its home shed, Exmouth Junction, on 5.12.64, a few months before the shed closed to steam.

Maurice Dart

Exmouth Junction shed on 24.5.53 with a comparison in motive power. Ex-LMS 1600 hp Diesel electric 10,000 stands beside locally shedded N class 2–6–0 31836. The two LMS diesels worked some services between Waterloo and Exeter in turn with SR diesel electrics 10201 and 10202.

The late Cedric Owen, the late Peter Tunks's Collection

In a line of withdrawn engines at Exmouth Junction shed on 7.4.63 is Z class 0–8–0T 30951. These powerful locos were designed for heavy yard shunting but ended their days banking at Exeter.

Maurice Dart

An Exmouth Junction-based 'Black Motor', 30691, a 700 class 0–6–0 stands outside the shed on 10.2.57.

Maurice Dart

'Strangers in the Camp' at Exmouth Junction on 22.12.63 are snowplough-fitted GWR 2251 class 0–6–0s 2214 and 2277, both shedded there. These locos replaced the 700 class 0–6–0s used for snow clearance the previous January. 2277 was withdrawn a few days after this photograph was taken, but 2214 survived until May 1965.

Maurice Dart

On 7.12.61 an 8750 class 0–6–0 PT, allocated to Wadebridge, while working the 6.58 a.m. train to Bodmin Road, was involved in a collision at Bodmin General. 4694 is outside Exmouth Junction shed on 31.12.61 *en route* to a loco works for repair. The engine subsequently returned to Wadebridge, but ended its days working from Exmouth Junction, being withdrawn in June 1965.

Maurice Dart

8750 class 0–6–0 PT 3679 was transferred from Swansea East Dock on to the Southern Region, working from Exmouth Junction, Feltham and Wadebridge sheds. It returned to Exmouth Junction from where it was withdrawn in April 1963 and is in the yard on 7.4.63.

Maurice Dart

Stored at Exmouth Junction on 22.12.63 is 6400 class 0–6–0 PT 6412, which had been used on the Seaton branch. It was later transferred to Gloucester. This engine has been preserved at Buckfastleigh.

Maurice Dart

A pair of T9 class 4–4–0s in store at Exmouth Junction shed with their chimneys 'capped' on 14.5.51 are 30706 and 30716 – their fine lines are apparent in this view.

Maurice Dart

An Exmouth-Junction 'Greyhound' T9 class 4–4–0 30717 stands outside the shed on 10.2.57, with another member of the class just inside. These engines put up consistently good performances on the Plymouth and North Cornwall lines, right up to their final years of service.

Maurice Dart

A classic design of 4–4–2T was the Adams 0415 class, known as 'Radial Tanks'. The three survivors were based at Exmouth Junction for working the Lyme Regis branch. In the yard on 22.3.59 is 30583, just returned from Eastleigh Loco Works. After withdrawal it was preserved on the Bluebell Railway. Note the drums of lubricating oil in the foreground and the mechanical coaling plant in the background.

Maurice Dart

A pair of Exmouth Junction-based 0–4–4T locos outside the shed on 10.2.57. They are M7 class 30323 and 02 class 30199.

Maurice Dart

The author has been unable to trace the history of this 'oddity', a four-wheeled petrol shunter which worked at Broad Clyst Sleeper Depot, where it was photographed from a passing train on 31.8.58. Having first been listed in Stock Books as 49S during 1947 it has a 'Heath Robinson' look about it, and was withdrawn during September 1959.

Maurice Dart

LMS 2MT 2–6–2T 41309 at Polsloe Bridge Halt with a train from Exmouth to Exeter Central. The engine appears to be carrying a 73E (Faversham) shedplate, but has been transferred to Exmouth Junction.

Maurice Dart Collection

138

Topsham with a 'goods' from Exmouth in charge of Exmouth Junction-based LMS 2MT 2–6–2T
41318.

Maurice Dart Collection

A pair of BR 3MT 2–6–2Ts with 82022 from Exmouth Junction shed in the lead at Lympstone with a
train for Exmouth. The 'double heading' was a method of working on extra engine to Exmouth,
saving a separate 'path'.

The late Peter Tunks's Collection

A pair of 2–6–2Ts from Exmouth Junction shed have just arrived at Exmouth, mid-morning on 11.6.62. BR 3MT 82025 is pilot to LMS 2MT 41308.

Maurice Dart

An M7 class 0–4–4T from Exmouth Junction shed, 30667, halts at Budleigh Salterton with a train from Exmouth to Tipton St Johns in June 1958.

Harry Cowan

Newton Poppleford in June 1958 with M7 class 0–4–4T 30025 on a train for Exmouth where the engine is sub-shedded.

Harry Cowan

M7 class 0–4–4T 30670 sub-shedded at Exmouth works an 'Up' goods through East Budleigh towards Tipton St Johns in June 1959.

Harry Cowan

On 11.5.63 BR 4MT 2–6–4T 80039 from Exmouth Junction shed brings a train for Exmouth into Tipton St Johns, the Junction for the lines to Sidmouth and Exmouth. Passenger services between Tipton St Johns and Exmouth ceased on 6.3.67, freight traffic having ended in 1964.

The late Peter Tunks's Collection

A BR 3MT 2–6–2T, possibly 82023, waits at Sidmouth with a train for Sidmouth Junction. The engine faces a climb of one mile at 1 in 54 to Bowd Summit followed by two miles downhill at 1 in 45 to Tipton St Johns. These engines would throw sparks out of the chimney while on the climb and the 'smuts' would fall back onto the cab roof, coming inside if the ventilator plate was open. Goods traffic to Sidmouth ceased on 27.1.64 with passengers lasting until 6.5.67.

The late Peter Tunks's Collection

Rebuilt 'Merchant Navy' class 4–6–2 35014 'Nederland Line' shedded at Nine Elms, runs into Sidmouth Junction with a Waterloo to Exeter express on 3.8.64.

Maurice Dart

An Exeter Central to Salisbury stopping train near Seaton Junction in charge of U class 2–6–0 31793 from Yeovil shed.

The late Peter Tunks's Collection

M7 class 0–4–4T 30048 at Seaton Junction on 11.6.62 with a motor train which it will propel to Seaton, where the engine is sub-shedded.

Maurice Dart

Following the transfer of various Southern Region lines to the Western Region, ex-GWR locos replaced SR types in places, such as on the Seaton branch. 6400 class 0–6–0 PT 6400 sub-shedded at Seaton departs from Seaton Junction for the terminus on 4.5.63.

The late Peter Tunks's Collection

Seaton Junction on 6.3.65 with the Seaton train in the branch platform in charge of ex-GWR 4800 class 0–4–2T 1442 hauling auto-coach W240W. This combination had taken over after diesel multiple units suffered failures the previous month, the engine working from Exmouth Junction shed as Seaton shed had closed on 4.11.63.

Michael Messenger

Colyton with a train being propelled to Seaton in charge of M7 class 0–4–4T 30021 in June 1960, the engine being sub-shedded at the terminus.

Harry Cowan

Colyford with the M7 0–4–4T from Seaton shed, 30021, waiting to proceed forward up the bank to Colyton and Seaton Junction in June 1960.

Harry Cowan

BR 3MT 2–6–2T 82017 from Exmouth Junction shed stands at Axminster, ready to depart with the 1.55 p.m. stopping train to Exeter Central on 3.7.58.

John Scrace, the late Peter Tunks's Collection

Seaton terminus and engine shed where M7 class 0–4–4T 30046 was kept. The train is waiting to start its return trip to Seaton Junction in June 1959. The branch closed to goods on 3.2.64 and to passengers on 7.3.66.

Harry Cowan

In heavy rain Adams 0415 class 4–4–2T 30583 stands at Axminster on 26.7.59 with the two-coach train for Lyme Regis, where the engine was sub-shedded. The branch was a 'light railway' and as such was restricted to a maximum speed of 25 mph. Leaving from the 'Up' side of Axminster station the line curved round in a semi-circle climbing at 1 in 80 to pass over the main line west of the station. This engine now lives on the Bluebell Railway.

Maurice Dart

LMS 2MT 2–6–2T 41307 shedded at Exmouth Junction enters Combpyne with a 'goods' working to Lyme Regis (which being in Dorset, does not feature in this book). The branch closed to goods from 3.2.64 and to passengers on 29.11.65.

The late Peter Tunks's Collection

No. 12, an 0–4–0ST built by the Avonside Engine Company in 1915, works number 1690, shunts in HM Dockyard at Devonport. This engine was used as a stationary boiler from 1957 until scrapped during 1959.

Mike Daly Collection

0–4–0ST's Peckett 784 of 1899 behind 783, inside Torycombe shed, at the bottom of the incline up to the village of Lee Moor, on 19.5.53. Steam working ceased in 1945 when the upper sections of the Lee Moor Tramway closed. Both engines are preserved, Lee Moor No. 2 (784) at Wheal Martyn Museum near St Austell with Lee Moor No. 1 (783) at Saltram House, near Plymouth. The gauge was 4 ft 6 in, known locally as 'The Dartmoor Gauge'.

Maurice Dart

One of the engines at Exeter Gas Works on 3.2.62. Peckett 0–4–0ST 2074 of 1946 shunts beside the Retort House in the plant. Rail traffic ceased in 1971 when the works closed. The loco is preserved at Buckfastleigh.

Richard Murrin